I HAVE A NAME

A VOICE CALLING OUT FROM THE WOMB

I HAVE A NAME
A VOICE CALLING OUT FROM THE WOMB

Copyright © 2021 by Shannen Palmore. All rights reserved. Printed in the United States of America

Edited and Published by SD Horton Enterprises

ISBN-13: 978-0-578-83012-4
Library of Congress Control Number (LCCN): 2020925708

All scriptures are taken from the New King James Version unless otherwise noted.

All rights reserved. Printed in the United States of America. No part of this publication may be reproduced, stored in a retrieval system, or transmitted in any form or by any means electronically, mechanically, photocopying, recording, or otherwise, without the prior written permission of the publisher except in the case of brief quotations embodied in critical articles and reviews.

Limit of Liability/Disclaimer of Warranty: While the publisher and author have used their best efforts in preparing this book, they make no representations or warranties with respect to the accuracy or completeness of the contents of this book and specifically disclaim any implied guarantees. The advice and strategies contained herein may not apply or be suitable for your situation. You should consult with a professional where appropriate. Neither the publisher or the author shall be liable for any loss or loss of profit or any other commercial damages, including but not limited to special, incidental, consequential, or other damages.

TABLE OF CONTENTS

Preface .... *i*

Special Thanks .... *ii*

Acknowledgments .... *iii*

Our Greatest Fear .... *iv*

Introduction ....*v*

Chapter 1: Birth 9

Chapter 2: Identity 17

Chapter 3: Mended 25

Chapter 4: Purposeless To Purposeful 31

Chapter 5: Moving Forward 37

Legacy Of An Adopted Child *41*

PREFACE

In 2016, the CDC reported 623,471 legal induced abortions by 48 reporting areas. The abortion rate for 2016 was 11.6 abortions per 1,000 women aged 15–44 years, and the abortion ratio was 186 abortions per 1,000 live births.

In this book, I want to tell part of my story. By sharing my experiences, I pray this will help those struggling to make a decision. My life has not been perfect, but I am grateful for every moment. I would like to speak up for every voice that has been unheard.

SPECIAL THANKS

I want to start by thanking my husband Quentin (Q). By the grace of God, he saw something in me that I didn't see in myself, and chose to walk through this journey with me. From the time of being 12 years old not wanting to share a pencil with him, until now with two children and a life I could never have imagined. I thank God for who He has given me and I look forward to the years to come.

I would like to also thank my parents. Their willingness and open-mindedness allowed me to be a part of a loving family. Growing up, I truly lacked nothing; and even as I have gotten older, I have grown to understand more and more of the different principles they instilled in me. I didn't always show my appreciation for them or even understand them at times, but I know they have always loved me and will continue to be there whenever I need them.

ACKNOWLEDGMENTS

I am forever grateful for my Pastor, Charles Bennett, III, and my First Lady, Talisha Bennett. You have blessed my life in ways you may never fully know. You have both helped me to change the perception about myself when I didn't even know it needed to be changed, and you both have been instrumental in my life.

A special thanks to my publishing company, SD Horton Enterprises. Thank you Elder Horton for helping me tremendously throughout the writing and publishing process.

OUR DEEPEST FEAR

Our deepest fear is not that we are inadequate.
Our deepest fear is that we are powerful beyond measure.
It is our light, not our darkness that most frightens us.
We ask ourselves
Who am I to be brilliant, gorgeous, talented, fabulous?
Actually, who are you not to be?
You are a child of God.

By: Marianne Williamson

INTRODUCTION

I REMEMBER THE NIGHT I SPENT IN A dumpster. I was dictated to by my own rebellion and it left me feeling alone. Dialing different phone numbers in my phone, I called for help and no one answered. I had a disagreement with my parents, so I left the house with rage in me and no place to go. If you have ever felt real rage, you'll know why I am using this exact wording.

Rage is a violent, uncontrollable anger. It comes from deep within and will unleash on anyone or anything if it's not kept in check. This wasn't something that developed overnight, but it was something that had been working in me; and it finally manifested itself because I allowed it to. When I left the house, my parents and I were not on good terms and I did not want to be found by them or potentially by the cops. There was nowhere to turn, so I looked for some sort of shelter. At this time, I lived in a much different climate than I do

INTRODUCTION

now. The temperature was dropping, and this was a place where you didn't want to be outside all night. As I started walking, I wasn't sure where to go; but I knew I didn't want to get snowed on. I could see my breath in the air. It was that cold!

I walked to an area where there were dumpsters, and as I said before, I didn't want to get caught. Looking back at this decision, I'm honestly at a loss about how it became the best one to make. Cold, tired, and even feeling down and out, I chose to get into one of the dumpsters. Thankfully, there were some boxes in there; so I laid on top of them. I never thought I would end up there, neither did I ever think I would be here today.

Unplanned, and at the time assumedly undefined, I was lost in a battle of who I was and Whose I was. Unlike most people, I was born knowing two mothers, one father, one sister, two brothers, and other siblings I knew about, but had not met (but felt the desire to meet). People generally see me as a bubbly, friendly person (who may or may not talk too much). There have been multiple occasions when people felt a bold urge to inform me that I was "too positive." Maybe this was and is true, but I don't foresee this changing. Only the few people who know me understand that things, both before I was born and throughout my life now, have tried

INTRODUCTION

to derail me at times; but I am still here by the grace of God.

"Before I formed you in the womb I knew you;
Before you were born I sanctified you".
Jeremiah 1:5

While most parents get to see a glimpse of their child during ultrasound visits, my parents didn't meet me until after I was born. Even though my parents got my name from a movie, I believe God put my name on their hearts and they gave me the name "Shannen." At the time, they did not know the meaning of my name and the importance it would have in my life. In the Hebrew language, Shannen means "God is gracious."

O how gracious He is, and hasn't stopped showing this throughout my life. The importance of a name has been undervalued and overlooked throughout time. This included me at one point. We have people naming their children without gaining an understanding or meaning of the names. Every time a name is spoken, you are also speaking its meaning. As I look back and see all the times God has been gracious to me, I think about the times I've overlooked those moments. So again, be mindful of what you are naming your children because every time you speak their name, you are speaking that meaning over them. I'm not going

INTRODUCTION

to tell you what to name your child, but maybe think twice about naming them something without considering whether or not the name would be edifying.

CHAPTER ONE

BIRTH

CHAPTER ONE

BIRTH

"Abortion is not just about a chance for you to have life; but the chance taken away from a child to experience one."

ACCORDING TO WOMENSHEALTH.GOV, "About 1 in 2 pregnancies in America are unplanned. Ideally, a woman who is surprised by an unplanned pregnancy is in good preconception health and is ready and able to care for a new child. But this sometimes isn't the case." Regardless of how an unplanned pregnancy has occurred, it is something a lot of women have faced. Each woman is faced with their own challenges in deciding what to do when they find out they have become pregnant, resulting in potential abortions.

While researching, I came across the Annual Abortion Statistics. Based on the state-level data, approximately 879,000 abortions took place in the

United States in 2017—down from approximately 892,000 abortions in 2016 and 913,000 abortions in 2015.
https://abort73.com/abortion_facts/us_abortion_statistics/

In 2004, the Guttmacher Institute anonymously surveyed 1,209 post-abortive women from nine different abortion clinics across the country. Of the women surveyed, 957 provided the main reason for having an abortion. This table lists each reason and the percentage of respondents who chose it.

Percentage	Reasons
<0.5%	Victim of rape
3%	Fetal health problems
4%	Physical health problems
4%	Would interfere with education or career
7%	Not mature enough to raise a child
8%	Don't want to be a single mother
19%	Done having children
23%	Can't afford a baby
25%	Not ready for a child
6%	Other

I HAVE A NAME

In 1992, unplanned, a woman became pregnant with a baby girl, and that baby girl was me. The notion of having a child was not on the agenda of my birth mom. At the age of 38 with a 21-year-old daughter and a 17-year-old son, starting over was not an option that she thought would be best suited for herself and everyone else.

Divided between her own maternal nature and the choice she was facing, she made a choice that would shape the course of my future. It had been six years into her journey where she was letting God guide her. She had been attending a church for only a short time before this happened, and I believe this played a part in her decision.

As a Believer, every life has value regardless of how it came to be, and she understood the importance of my life. The decision was made to go through with the pregnancy knowing the risks involved. Towards the end of the pregnancy, she was diagnosed with toxemia, also known as preeclampsia. Preeclampsia "is a condition unique to human pregnancy. It is diagnosed by the elevation of the expectant mother's blood pressure usually after the 20th week of pregnancy" (Preeclampsia Foundation). The effects on mothers can be liver damage, kidney damage, possibly lead to brain damage, and even sometimes can cause death to the

CHAPTER ONE: BIRTH

mother and infant. With the knowledge of preeclampsia and all of the different medical conditions, the decision was made to induce labor 6 weeks early.

Not only did she have a reason for abortion that is accepted by much of our current culture, but she also had medical reasons on top of that. This was in 1993 mind you. There has been major headway in this area to help protect mothers and their unborn children; but at that time it was something that was even more detrimental to both mother and child. On March 16, 1993, I was born prematurely, and was given the name Sarah, meaning "princess." Anytime there is an unplanned pregnancy, there are doubts, questions, and fears; and ultimately with that, the decision was made to not keep me. Going through one of the most unselfish acts, she decided to give me up for adoption. Before she had me, the thought that she would not be able to keep me was a burden. Knowing in the end it would be what was best for me, she gave me a chance for a better life.

With this knowledge, as well as the consent of her children, she sought out who she thought would be the best choice of parents for me. She considered multiple couples/families until she found mine. By the time I was born, she had chosen a family with whom I would be raised. Today, almost 60%-70% of domestic adoptions are now open adoptions, which means there is a degree of openness and disclosure of information between adoptive and birth parents regarding the adopted child. https://adoptionnetwork.com/adoption-statistics.

Some common misconceptions involving adopting are, the children are mad at their biological parents for not keeping them; not being able to see the child once given up for adoption; the child not knowing they were adopted; only irresponsible mothers place their children up for adoption; adoption agencies withhold information; and more.

I use the term "misconceptions" because these things have occurred, but very rarely. It has been found that mothers who still have contact with their child they gave up for adoption have had a better time coping with the reality of it. Child adoption statistics show that over 90% of adopted children ages 5 and older have positive feelings about their adoption. I'm sharing this information, not as a form of judgment, but as a way to show that there is another way despite why or how a pregnancy came to be.

I was brought into a home with 2 loving parents and 3 siblings (2 of whom were also adopted). My parents not only opened their home, but also their hearts to children who ultimately became their own. They loved us all exactly the same as if we came through them.

CHAPTER ONE: BIRTH

While growing up, these differences were never a big concern for us. The oldest sibling was my sister, who was the only biological one in the family, and was Caucasian. Then, my oldest brother was Hispanic, and my other brother was a quarter African-American. I remember going to school, and the kids would ask me why my skin was darker than theirs. I would cry when I got home, not understanding how very different I was…and not just in color. When I would go home, I would ask my mom, "What should I tell these children?" I really didn't know what color I was, or what the term "race" meant at the time.

I always thought I just tanned better. My mother would tell me to tell the other kids that I drank too much chocolate milk. Looking at it, that may seem cute, but I believe it was the start of me being uncomfortable in my own skin. Eventually, I would come to the knowledge of who I was and Whose I am.

CHAPTER TWO

IDENTITY

CHAPTER TWO

IDENTITY

"You even formed every bone in my body when you created me in the secret place, carefully, skillfully shaping me from nothing to something. You saw who you created me to be before I became me! Before I'd ever seen the light of day, the number of days you planned for me were already recorded in your book".
Psalms 139:15

I DIDN'T EVEN TAKE ENOUGH TO END MY life! There was a time when I didn't know a way out of my feelings. Selfishly, I didn't want to deal with anything or anyone, and I decided I was done. Looking back, I only remember bits and pieces. I remember having my phone in my hand, but I don't remember if I actually called someone or not. I do remember taking the pills though.

In a brief moment of despair, I gave it all up. It was an ill-conceived attempt at suicide. Had I followed

CHAPTER TWO: IDENTITY

through with the attempt, the impact would've been irreversible. It was a failed effort, and I don't think I actually wanted to die. I just wanted the pain to stop.

At one point, I even tried cutting to cope with the pain. I took a bobby pin, took off the rubber end, and I cut the word "freedom" into my left arm. I wanted to be free from people's perception of me. I wanted to be free to be who I really was. All I could see was how bad I felt everything was, instead of how things could be. By the grace of God, I am still here. There was a deeply rooted internal conflict that would take years to overcome. Not knowing who I was, and how I sought to find out would ultimately lead me to being lost. I defined myself by what I assumed those around me thought of me instead of looking at the source of who I was.

It was confusing at the time because I had other influences around me telling me what I should and shouldn't be. I was being relegated by skin color rather than to who God created me to be. My priorities were jacked up and the people I put on a pedestal were the ones who were feeding into my instability, both emotionally and mentally.

I was not confident in who I was at all. I would try to fit in and often find myself feeling alone. Reaching out to the wrong crowd, I got into some trouble. I went to a predominantly Caucasian school with some color splashed into the mixture. When I would hang out with my white friends, I was considered the black one in the group. When I would hang out with my black friends, I was the white one. I only wanted to just be me, which at this point was lost in the confusion.

I came to the conclusion that I wasn't black or white. I was just me. When I tried to explain that it got lost in translation. One of my last meetings with my guidance counselor was him saying to me (concerning graduating high school), "if you graduate…" Keep in mind, I was a good student with decent grades at the time. There were a few classes with which I struggled, but there was no real indication of me not graduating other than the color of my skin. I got myself into a situation that I instantly regretted and did not know a way out of.

I think dealing with sexual abuse, or any form of abuse is challenging; but putting the blame on yourself is one of the most poisonous things you can do.

To be honest, I don't know if putting or finding someone to blame is really helpful either. I have found dozens of reasons to blame myself, the persons who committed the act, as well as people I thought somehow

CHAPTER TWO: IDENTITY

should have been there for me when I was hurting.

I find in a lot of cases victims blame themselves. Questions and thoughts would arise like, "I should've seen this coming, I shouldn't have been out so late, maybe if I would've just spoken up more, I shouldn't have been afraid, how could I let this happen to myself?" These questions and thoughts will continue to be with you until you decide to not allow them by releasing the desire to carry them any longer.

For some, it takes longer than others, but it is possible to not carry that weight around. I know because I was burdened down with these questions for years. I brought an impossible situation to people who quite possibly would've never had to face otherwise. To expect people to know all the right things to say or do in every situation is not rational.

Being faced with the fact that your child was sexually assaulted, and at this point, there was nothing you could do to protect them from it, is a pain and reality I would never want to face. As I continue to learn this thing called parenting, I could only imagine a child of mine coming to me with information such as this. For a long time, I was angry at myself, as well as those around me.

I HAVE A NAME

Somehow, I thought being angry would help the pain; but it did not.

It festered until I exploded with most of what happened. I couldn't bring myself to reveal the whole story. To be honest, I don't think I ever did. Between guilt, shame, and hurt, I've only shared the whole story with one person other than God.

To cope with everything, I started drinking. I would only drink small amounts out of different bottles so as to not get caught. I eventually had "friends" from whom I would buy it. I don't remember why, but one day I decided that drinking at night was not good enough. So, I drank the next day too. The only issue with that was I was in school. I didn't get caught the day of, but I did get caught the day after. They searched my backpack and went through everything to find a small bottle of alcohol.

As a result, I got in-school suspension and eventually led me to juvie (Juvenile Detention). To this day, I hate thinking about that place. When you walk, you are told to look down and not make eye contact with other kids. You had to walk against a wall when other groups were passing, and it was belittling and a dehumanizing experience

CHAPTER TWO: IDENTITY

I understand juvie is not meant to be fun, but it did not make sense to me and still does not make sense to me. Instead of teaching kids better ways of dealing with things and giving them tools, everything was stripped away, including your dignity. I was there for a brief time, and I remember the judge sitting there looking at me with her cold, dark eyes. She had no compassion and no idea what I went through to get to be in that position, and nor did she care.

At the time, I did not truly understand the essence of my identity. With all that had been transpiring, I was only able to catch glimpses of my true identity. Only over the past few years have I truly started to understand the meaning behind identity, and in Who and what my identity resides in. It was said by my pastor, Pastor Bennett, that "your identity does not come from what you do, but who you are and really who created you."

CHAPTER THREE

MENDED

CHAPTER THREE

MENDED

"For I know the plans I have for you,' declares the Lord, 'plans to prosper you and not to harm you, plans to give you hope and a future."
Jeremiah 29:11

SILENCE HAS NEVER BEEN MORE deafening. Unable to speak, unable to convey; unable to do anything but enter the abyss of eternity, children slip away. As believers, we believe our children are spared and go to Heaven; however they are unable to experience life. I can't help but to think about all these children that are unborn due to abortions and they never got the chance to live. So many voices are being heard, except the ones of those not living. I can't imagine being the one in a position to face a pregnancy that is medically threatening; being young, not having support, or other reasons that add to the challenge of any pregnancy.

CHAPTER THREE: MENDED

Talking with my birth mom, I caught a glimpse into the world of someone who experienced an unplanned pregnancy. She would tell me how I was a gift from God, and how much she loved me, and how giving me up was one of the hardest things she ever did.

Although I "came to be" unintentionally, I believe God had an intentional plan for me. As she continued to seek God, He continued to give her peace, and helped her through the various challenges she faced. There were times she struggled with depression, and when her husband passed she fell into despair. Unconnected and estranged, we lost touch. Somewhere between my phone calls to her, I had made a decision that I was not going to be abandoned again.

I understood she was hurting, but I felt like one of the only people in my life who actually understood me had abandoned me, just like others did. On the road to a better relationship, I remember telling her that there had to be a decision made; either you're in my life or you're not. I couldn't bear any more pain. With that decision, we were able to talk and she chose to remain in my life;

and once again, our relationship began to blossom. And I again felt at peace with the woman who dared to not only muster the strength to have me, but also the courage to give me up for adoption. A short time before she passed, I became pregnant with my son Roman. I told my adoptive mom about the pregnancy, and I was waiting to tell my birth mom. I had planned on telling her, but I never got the chance. In April of 2016, I felt a pain that I never imagined existed.

I remember it like it was yesterday. I woke up and had received multiple messages from my half-sister and my aunt saying I needed to call them. Somehow, I already felt like I knew what the news was about. Looking back at it now, I think maybe it was the Holy Spirit preparing me. I still got ready for work and started praying.

I remember praying in the shower and just crying out to God for the pain I was feeling to go away. It wasn't until I got to work that my sister called and told me my mom had passed. In the back room at work, I fell to my knees confirming what I already knew. She went with

CHAPTER THREE: MENDED

love and a relationship with Jesus, and left a legacy that is still being created. During the day, I would be fine. I would keep distracted. But at night, there was nowhere to hide. Gripped by a heart-wrenching pain, I would cry myself to sleep praying and knowing God was my comforter.

My husband would hold me tight trying to ease my pain, and even though I would cry, I didn't forget that God had me. I knew the pain would cease and I would get through as long as I stayed focused on Him.

Up to this time, I had only talked to my sister a few times and didn't have much of a relationship with her, and I didn't really know anyone else. God had me in the palms of His hands and I just wanted to stay in them. I decided not to go to the funeral and I knew it would not bring her back. Looking back at it, I still feel like I made the right decision. I remember people reaching out to me over Facebook doing their best to encourage me by telling me, "at least you have another mom."

So here's the thing, I love both of my moms, but

they are very different and exhibit love in their own way. God healed me from my pain and continues to help keep me focused. It is an ongoing thing. Anyone who has ever lost someone knows that there is a balance of remembering the person, missing them, and not letting it take hold of you. There are times I still cry, but I continue to seek God and He keeps me.

CHAPTER FOUR

PURPOSELESS TO PURPOSEFUL

CHAPTER FOUR

PURPOSELESS TO PURPOSEFUL

"For You formed my inward parts; You covered me in my mother's womb."
Psalms 139:13 NKJV

LOOKING AT MY STORY, I SEE WHERE I started as Sarah, and then became Shannen. I have a name but I am more than it. I am a child of God. He cares and tends to me as such. He sees our tears and erases fears. What a Mighty God we serve!

I didn't begin my journey to self-worth and healing until long after everything occurred. One night while reflecting with my husband, I realized I never

CHAPTER FOUR: PURPOSELESS TO PURPOSEFUL

really started healing until we had already been married for a couple of years. Man, God blessed me with such a wonderful husband, "my holy hookup." That kind of pain could be lethal to marriage, and potentially fatal.

By the grace of God, I gave myself fully to Him so He could really start working in me. Little by little, my confidence grew - not just in looks, but how I truly felt about and saw myself. I have to stay surrendered daily.

I was no longer the abandoned little girl who didn't know who she was or where she fits in. When I found God, or better yet He found me, it literally changed my life. Over time, God would begin to pull away the hurt, shame, and guilt that I carried with me. I would begin to see myself the same way He saw me. One day, I was just crying at the altar. This happened on multiple occasions, and I just sensed God taking the shame, regrets, fears, and abandonment. I didn't have to have them anymore. Pastor called for me, and I remember him telling me that I was no longer abandoned or an orphan. I no longer had to live like I didn't belong somewhere, and I was home.

> *The orphan spirit operates out of insecurities and jealousy, tries to earn love, tries to medicate his deep internal alienation through physical stimulation, is driven by the need for success, uses people as objects to fulfill their goals, repels their children, has issues with anger and fits of rage, always in competition with others, has a lack of self-esteem, receives their primary identity through material possessions, their physical appearance, and activities. - 13 Traits of 'Orphan Spirit' Leaders — Charisma News*

This broken mentality has ensnared so many, both knowingly and unknowingly. There will always be things in our control and things we cannot control. One thing remains: The way we let the things outside of us affect us.

You know you don't always see the value in a gift until it's revealed to you. I appreciated my mom, but until I had Roman, I did not fully understand just how much I valued her. I have been gifted with a child who has taught me so much. It has helped me to catch a glimpse of how much God loves us. One time, after having to discipline Roman, I was distraught. I didn't want to hurt him or to allow any harm to come to him.

CHAPTER FOUR: PURPOSELESS TO PURPOSEFUL

After I disciplined him, I remember just wanting to hold and comfort him. I didn't just scoop him up. I waited and he came to me and said 'sorry' the best way he could. I told him that I already forgave him and just held him. This was one of the many lessons God has shown me through my son. When we do wrong, if we just go to our Father, we realize that He has already forgiven us and just wants to care for us. Forgiveness is for you and not always for the other person. You can disagree with someone and still forgive them. To forgive exhibits strength while not forgiving exhibits weakness.

It can be harder to forgive someone rather than hang on to the resentment; but forgiveness results in a far greater outcome. Relationships can be restored and hearts can be healed. Whether or not that person has earned forgiveness in your eyes does not deem them unforgiveable. My confidence didn't come from my own abilities. It came from who God said I was. Living a life full of purpose is really the only way to live. Otherwise, we are the walking dead. Almost in a zombie-like state, we just go from one place or thing to another not really impacting those around in a meaningful or purposeful manner. Whereas a life of purpose gives us direction, as well as a purpose to live, love, and grow. What I once saw as just life, or you only live once (YOLO), I now see as only the beginning. As a believer, this is not the only life we have. Maybe here on this Earth, but not in eternity. Everything we do makes a difference during and after we leave this Earth.

CHAPTER FIVE

MOVING FORWARD

CHAPTER FIVE

MOVING FORWARD

SO OFTEN, PEOPLE WOULD COME UP to me and say how blessed I am. I do not disagree; however, a wise man said, "Never judge someone's harvest without knowing their seed" *(Bishop, Dr. Mikel Brown)*. People see me where I am now and I am grateful that I am here. However, not everyone has seen or knows the different challenges I have faced or the obstacles God has helped me overcome. I've already shared with you various parts, including struggling with alcohol, suicide, depression, anxiety, sexual abuse, emotional abuse, and just baggage. By the grace of God, when I look in the mirror, I no longer see all that. The more time I spend

CHAPTER FIVE: MOVING FORWARD

with God, the more I start to see myself as I am and not who I was or what I was doing. I still have questions and I still go to God with them.

Writing, as it turns out, can be very therapeutic. I didn't realize that writing all of this would add to the healing that has already taken place. As I worked through putting words onto each page, I had to deal with different thoughts, emotions, times, and places I didn't necessarily want to think about. By writing this all out, I was forced to embrace the areas I still had pushed to the side and appreciate the areas that I have overcome. This has truly been an experience, and I'm only at the beginning. I believe this will help me to mend and help me to move forward in ways I never thought possible.

When I first started writing my story it was my husband, my son, and me. Now, we have 2 sons and are continuing to grow daily. At the beginning of this journey of writing my story, I was different than I am now. The way I love and live have changed, and I would say for the better.

My shoulds are now musts, my ifs are now

whens, and I am continuing to seek God daily. There are people he have strategically been placed in my life who help me beyond what words can express. If I started naming them all, I would have to create a separate book.

He who finds his life will lose it, and he who loses his life for My sake will find it.
Matthew 10:39 NKJV

Life is a gift, but we determine how to live it. I feel like I was given an exceptional gift; and although at times I've undervalued it, I am grateful for all God has done in me and through me. Our past doesn't define us. Our future does.

Because of the choices that were made...
I Have A Name.

LEGACY OF AN ADOPTED CHILD
(Author Unknown)

Once there were two women
Who never knew each other.
One you do not remember,
The other you call mother.
Two different lives
Shaped to make yours one.
One became your guiding star,
The other became your sun.
The first gave you life
And the second taught you to live it.
The first gave you a need for love
And the second was there to give it.
One gave you a nationality,
The other gave you a name.
One gave you a seed of talent,
The other gave you an aim
One gave you emotions,
The other calmed your fears.
One saw your first sweet smile,
The other dried your tears.

One gave you up --
It was all that she could do.
The other prayed for a child
And God led her straight to you.
And now you ask me
Through your tears,
The age-old question
Through the years:
Heredity or environment
Which are you the product of?
Neither, my darling -- neither,
Just two different kinds of love"

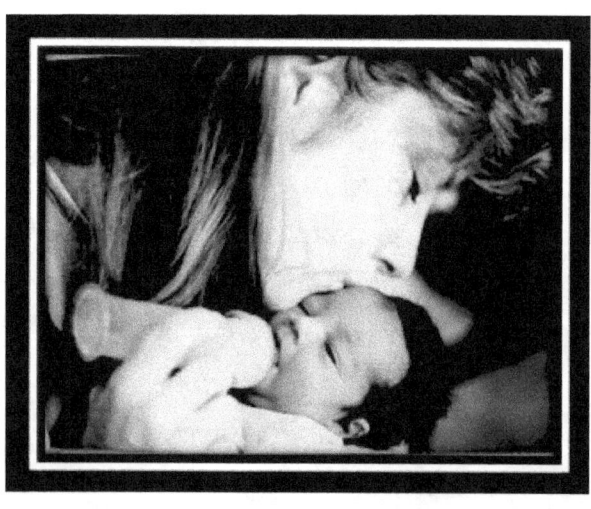

$8.95
ISBN 978-0-578-83012-4

www.ingramcontent.com/pod-product-compliance
Lightning Source LLC
Chambersburg PA
CBHW071845290426
44109CB00017B/1929